Let Freedom Ring

The Oregon Trail

by Elizabeth D. Jaffe

Consultant:
The National Oregon/California Trail Center
Montpelier, Idaho

Bridgestone Books
an imprint of Capstone Press
Mankato, Minnesota

Bridgestone Books are published by Capstone Press,
151 Good Counsel Drive • P.O. Box 669 • Mankato, Minnesota 56002.
www.capstonepress.com

Printed in the United States of America

Library of Congress Cataloging-in-Publication Data
Jaffe, Elizabeth Dana.
    The Oregon Trail / by Elizabeth D. Jaffe.
        p. cm. — (Let freedom ring)
    Includes bibliographical references and index.
    Summary: Examines the famous westward route of American settlement during the 1800s, including everyday life on the trail, what it took to make the journey successfully, and what happened to unsuccessful attempts to reach the Oregon Territory.
    ISBN 0-7368-1101-X (hardcover)
    ISBN 0-7368-4508-9 (paperback)
    1. Oregon National Historic Trail—History—Juvenile literature. 2. Overland journeys to the Pacific—Juvenile literature. 3. Pioneers—West (U.S.)—History—19th century—Juvenile literature. 4. Frontier and pioneer life—West (U.S.)—Juvenile literature. 5. West (U.S.)—History—19th century—Juvenile literature. [1. Oregon National Historic Trail. 2. Overland journeys to the Pacific. 3. Frontier and pioneer life—West (U.S.). 4. West (U.S.)—History—19th century.] I. Title. II. Series.
F597 .J36 2002
917.804'2—dc21   2001003428

Editorial Credits
Charles Pederson, editor; Kia Bielke, cover designer, interior layout designer, and illustrator; Jennifer Schonborn, cover production designer and illustrator; Deirdre Barton, photo researcher

Photo Credits
Cover: Library of Congress/John Charles Frémont (right), Hulton/Archive Photos (middle), Stockbyte (left); Stockbyte, 4, 10, 16, 26, 34, 38; Smithsonian American Art Museum, Washington, D.C./Art Resource, NY, 5, 29; North Wind Picture Archives, 6, 24, 27, 32; Lake County Museum/CORBIS, 9; Hulton/Archive Photos, 12, 35, 36; Peter Harholdt/CORBIS, 15; PhotoSphere Images, 17, 20–21, 39, 42, 43; Richard Thom/Visuals Unlimited, 18; N. Carter/North Wind Picture Archives, 23; Levi Strauss & Co., 30; CORBIS, 40

1   2   3   4   5   6   07   06   05   04   03   02

Table of Contents

Chapter One

Wandering the Wilds

Imagine a person who leaves everything behind to walk 2,000 miles (3,200 kilometers) through prairie heat, dust storms, or icy mountain air. That person crosses rivers and mountains. The person is thirsty, starved, dirty, and sick, but the hope of a western paradise keeps the person going.

Many emigrants made journeys like this in the 1800s over the Oregon Trail, or Oregon-California Trail. Emigrants leave one place to go live in another place. About 160,000 emigrants left the eastern United States to move west to Oregon and surrounding areas.

The Louisiana Purchase

In 1803, the U.S. government bought the Louisiana Territory from France for about $15 million. The land lay west of the Mississippi River. Through the purchase, the United States gained

As in this painting, many emigrants traveling to Oregon imagined that the West would be a kind of paradise.

825,000 square miles (2.1 million square kilometers) of land from the Mississippi River to the Rocky Mountains.

Also in 1803, U.S. president Thomas Jefferson asked Meriwether Lewis and William Clark to explore the territory. They were to find an all-water route from the Missouri River to the Pacific Ocean.

Lewis and Clark traveled up the Missouri River and across the Rocky Mountains. They finally reached the Pacific Ocean, but no all-water route existed. They did bring back maps and notes about the area that helped later travelers find their way.

In 1804, Lewis and Clark (background, in brown and blue coats) set out to find a water route to the Pacific Ocean. Here they speak with American Indians.

Mountain Men

Even after Lewis and Clark's notes were published, few people headed west. Most of those who did were adventurers or wanted to escape the crowded East. They were called mountain men. The West was rich in furs, and many mountain men became fur traders and trappers.

Mountain men explored western areas that became important to travelers. In 1824, Jedediah Smith rediscovered South Pass, in today's southern Idaho. Earlier explorers had kept the pass secret. Smith made sure everyone knew about it. In 1832, Joe Walker and Benjamin Bonneville opened a trail to California that emigrants later followed. Beginning in 1842, John Frémont wrote about several expeditions that made the trip seem easy and enjoyable.

Around 1850, James Beckwourth, a former slave, discovered what is now called Beckwourth Pass in the Sierra Nevada Mountains. The pass opened a route to California's Sacramento Valley.

People heard of good farmland in the West. But families ran most farms. The trip to Oregon was still considered too dangerous for families.

In Need of a Better Life

Early in the 1800s, America and Britain wanted Oregon. They agreed that people of both countries could occupy Oregon. They further agreed that Oregon would later belong to the country with the most people living there.

For that reason, the United States offered free land to people moving west in the mid-1800s. Free land meant opportunities for a better life, wealth, and independence.

Emigrants headed West for many reasons. In 1837, hard times hit the United States and people lost their jobs. Small farmers could not compete with larger farmers. Overcrowded eastern cities were full of disease and unclean conditions. People saw the wild areas of the West as a chance for a new, better life. Oregon and its rich farmland looked more promising all the time.

Carrying Religion

Marcus and Narcissa Whitman were among the first emigrants to travel to Oregon in a covered wagon.

Religious Emigrants

Religious beliefs prompted some people to move west. One of the largest religious groups to emigrate west was the Mormons, or the Church of Jesus Christ of Latter-day Saints. In the East, many people disliked Mormon beliefs and threatened to kill the Mormons. In 1846–1847, Mormon leader Brigham Young (right) guided a group to Utah. By 1870, more than 80,000 Mormons had moved to Utah.

They were missionaries, whose goal was to turn the American Indians to Christianity.

In 1836, the Whitmans traveled to the Oregon area with other missionaries. Their journey inspired many emigrants to head for Oregon. The Whitmans later guided large groups along the Oregon Trail.

Chapter Two

Preparations for the Trip

The Whitmans led the Great Migration to Oregon in 1843. About 1,000 emigrants made that first journey. Thousands more emigrants followed in later years. The trail that they followed crossed modern-day Missouri, Kansas, Nebraska, Wyoming, Idaho, and Oregon.

The Oregon Trail began at several jumping-off cities on the Missouri River. Emigrants could prepare and then start their journey at these cities. Emigrants bought supplies and made other preparations to leave. The most popular jumping-off city was Independence, Missouri.

Many emigrants made their needed purchases at their jumping-off city. They often bought dry goods instead of fresh foods that easily spoiled. Some families sold everything they owned to make the trip, hoping life would be better in a new land.

49th Parallel

Columbia River

★ Oregon City

Continental Divide

Missouri River

OREGON

IDAHO

CALIFORNIA

WYOMING

Donner Pass

★ Montpelier, ID

South Pass

■ Independence Rock

SIERRA NEVADA MOUNTAINS

ROCKY MOUNTAINS

■ Chimney Rock

★ Sutter's Fort

NEVADA

Hastings "Shortcut"

UTAH

NEBRASKA

Pacific Ocean

KANSAS

★ Independence

MISSOURI

N
W   E
S

Scale

| 50 | 100 | 150 | 200 |
| 100 | 200 | 300 |
meters

Key
----- Oregon-California Trail
----- Oregon Trail
----- California Trail

The Oregon Trail

Emigrant families crossed the prairies, rivers, and
mountains of Missouri, Kansas, Nebraska, Wyoming,
and Idaho to reach Oregon. The map above also
shows the California part of the trail.

11

Emigrants bought many things at their jumping-off city. They could buy flour, bacon, beans, dried meat, coffee, sugar, and salt at their jumping-off city. Travelers also needed medical supplies, cooking tools, weapons, blankets, and clothes.

Most people bought a team of four to six oxen to pull a prairie schooner. Oxen were slow but reliable and patient. They could live on grass alone, so emigrants did not have to buy or carry food for them.

Snow in the mountains sometimes trapped travelers who left their jumping-off city too late in the year.

Ships of the Prairie

Emigrants usually traveled in covered wagons known as prairie schooners. A schooner is a type of ship, and with their white canvas covers, these wagons looked like ships.

A prairie schooner was about 10 feet (3 meters) tall and 5 feet (1.5 meters) wide. The covering was made of waterproof canvas that the emigrants could pull closed to keep out rain, dust, and wind.

Riding in the wagon was uncomfortable, and walking was usually easier. In most cases, the emigrants' goods filled the space inside the wagon, so there was little choice but to walk.

The Perfect Time to Leave

With preparations complete, emigrants had to wait for the perfect time to start their journey. If they left too early, spring rain might flood the trail. Emigrants would then spend most of their time digging themselves out of the mud. They also had to wait for the grass to grow so their animals would have food along the way. If emigrants waited too long, they might get caught in early-winter snows later in the trip. Most people left their jumping-off city in April or May.

It was difficult for a poor family to afford taking the trail. In the mid-1800's, the Oregon Trail trip cost as much as $1,500. Travelers needed extra money to replace, fix, or buy needed items that had risen in price. Travelers needed money to pay for bridge or ferry crossings at rivers.

The Group

Emigrants needed to know their fellow travelers. Groups sometimes already knew each other. At other times, groups met for the first time at their jumping-off city. The best groups included people with different skills, such as a doctor, hunter, and carpenter. Group members helped and protected each other along the way.

Group organization was important. Many emigrants wrote rules for different situations. Most groups elected a captain to lead them and to make sure people followed the rules. The trail was not easy to follow in the first few years. Many groups hired guides who knew western lands. These guides could lead groups safely to Oregon or California.

Going by Ship

Going overland by covered wagon was not the only way to reach the West. Emigrants could board a ship that might have looked like the one below. The boat trip from the East Coast around South America to Oregon was about 13,000 miles (21,000 kilometers) long. At $300 per person, the trip was too expensive for many families and could take from six months to a full year. The food on ships was awful, and ships were crowded and dirty. Passengers hoped their ship would not sink before it reached Oregon.

Chapter Three

At Home on the Trail

Each trip on the Oregon Trail was different from all others. Every group had different experiences. However, many trips had a routine.

Each day began before sunrise. Breakfast was usually coffee and bacon. By 7:00 in the morning, the wagons were ready for the day's journey.

Lunch was coffee, cold beans, and leftovers from breakfast. At sunset, the travelers circled their wagons for the night. The circle served as a campsite, a place for their animals, and protection from wild animals.

After circling the wagons, the travelers sat down for a dinner of tea, rice, bacon, or dried beef. Sometimes, the travelers might catch fish or shoot buffalo or other animals. When they could not make a fire, emigrants ate their food cold.

At night, the travelers played instruments, sang, and told stories. Children sometimes had school lessons.

Covered wagons like those in this reenactment were a common means of transportation for emigrants. At night, emigrants drew their wagons into a circle as protection from wild animals.

Most people slept on the ground. Sleeping was uncomfortable, but after walking all day, most people did not care. A guard stayed awake watching for danger. Many people slept with guns nearby. Before sunrise, the schedule began again.

Some travelers considered Sunday a day of rest. Many trains did not travel on Sunday. People and animals could relax. Men could hunt, fish, or repair items. Women could wash clothing if water was near. Some trains, however, did not want to lose travel time by stopping on Sunday. They might have worship services in the morning, then move on.

Some travelers scratched their names and the date of their trip on Independence Rock (right) to mark their passage.

Traffic

Wagons traveled in a single line. From a distance, the line looked like a train, so the groups were called wagon trains. In earlier years, wagon trains might be a few wagons long. As the number of emigrants grew, longer wagon trains formed.

Every day, a different wagon got a chance to be in front. This wagon could avoid the blinding, choking dust that oxen and other wagons stirred up. If a wagon's occupants took too long to get ready in the morning, they missed their place in line and had to travel at the back for the day.

Landmarks

Landmarks were important on the journey. They showed how far travelers had come. Wagon trains then knew they were headed the right way.

Travelers passed several landmarks on the trip. One landmark was a tall column of rock emigrants called Chimney Rock. Emigrants then passed Courthouse Rock. Some wagon trains reached Independence Rock on July 4, Independence Day. Many emigrants considered it the halfway mark to Oregon, though it was a bit less than half.

In the Rockies, travelers reached South Pass, the real halfway point. South Pass marked the Continental Divide. On one side, rivers flowed west toward the Pacific Ocean. On the other side, rivers flowed east toward the Mississippi River. At South Pass, travelers had to choose to head northwest to Oregon or southwest to Utah or California.

Overcoming Barriers

Travelers had to overcome many barriers, including rivers. Some rivers were shallow, and wagons could ride across. Emigrants might build a raft, or they might remove the wagon wheels and float the wagon across. It could take an hour for a wagon to cross a river and five days for an entire wagon train.

At major river crossings, some emigrants used ferries. Travelers had to pay for ferry rides and then patiently wait several days for their turn to cross.

Fast rivers swept away many wagons. Some wagons tipped or broke apart in the current. Near the end of the trail, the rough rapids of the Columbia River provided one of the most dangerous river stretches. Only later did a land route open that went around the Columbia.

Mountains were a major barrier. Animals and people could haul wagons up. Going down was more difficult because wagons had no brakes and could easily begin to roll out of control.

To avoid runaway wagons, travelers tied a rope from the back of a wagon to a tree or rock. They then lowered the wagon. They sometimes jammed logs beneath the wheels to slow the wagon.

Reenactors show the way emigrants crossed rivers on the trail.

Many people emptied their wagon or cut it in half before lowering it. Others found that crossing the mountain was too hard. These people left their wagons behind and continued without them. The steepest downward part of the trail was at Big Hill, near modern Montpelier, Idaho.

Food became scarce as the trip went on, and some emigrants nearly starved to death. Drinkable water was as hard to find as good food, especially near the Rockies. Some people and animals drank any water, even if it was unhealthy.

Accidents

Accidents were common. Accidents often happened to children, because parents could not always watch them closely. Wagons ran over many children. Some children wandered off from trains and were lost or left behind.

The Oregon Trail has been called the longest graveyard in the United States. About 20,000 people died along the trail.

There were so many hardships along the trail that about one out of 10 emigrants returned to the East. These people were called go-backs.

Cholera

Diseases killed thousands on the Oregon Trail, and cholera was one of the worst. It grew in the trail's unclean conditions. Cholera, the "unseen destroyer," could kill quickly. A person might feel fine in the morning, be ill at noon, and die by evening. Emigrants buried their dead along the trail and left stones to mark the graves.

American Indians

Emigrants feared American Indians, but many tribes were helpful and friendly. Each tribe's relationship with the emigrants was different, but most tribes liked the opportunity to trade. Emigrants traded clothes, tobacco, or rifles for American Indians' horses, food, or moccasins. Tribes along the trail included the Pawnee, Sioux, Shoshone, Blackfoot, Cheyenne, Crow, and Bannock.

Over the years, emigrants' diseases wiped out some tribes. Also, by the late 1850s, emigrants' animals had overgrazed prairie lands. The emigrants had burned the firewood and killed the buffalo. Because of these conditions, some tribes starved or had to beg or steal food.

As emigrants settled on the land, American Indians reacted more violently. They sometimes fought wagon trains or attacked settlements in their area. In all, however, American Indians killed fewer than 400 travelers to Oregon.

This drawing shows a Mandan village in the early 1800s. The Mandans were one group that traded with emigrants.

Amelia Stewart Smith's Diary

Hardships were common to emigrants on the trail. In 1853, emigrant Amelia Stewart Smith wrote about her troubles during the trip. Here are a few diary entries:

July 22nd: "[Our son] Chat had a very narrow escape from being run over . . . Somehow he kept from under the wheels and escaped with only a good, or I should say, a bad scare."

August 7th: "The roads have been very dusty, no water, nothing but dust and . . . the odor from dead cattle."

August 8th: "We left, unknowingly, our [daughter] Lucy behind. Not a soul had missed her until we had gone some [distance] . . . Just then another train drove up behind us, with Lucy. She was terribly frightened and so were some more of us when we learned what a narrow escape she had run."

September 8th: "Traveled 14 miles [22 kilometers] over the worst road that was ever made, up and down, very steep . . . Now we are on the end of a log, now over a big root of a tree. Now bounce down in a mud hole, then bang goes the other side of the wagon, and woe be to whatever is inside."

Chapter Four

Choosing California

During the 1840s, increasing numbers of emigrants chose California over Oregon. At South Pass, the California Trail split off from the Oregon Trail. California-bound emigrants headed south across northwestern Utah and Nevada. They continued through the Sierra Nevada Mountains and into California. Travelers needed to go as fast as possible to avoid early snows high in the Sierra Nevada Mountains.

Discovering Gold

The main reason people began to head to California was for gold. A carpenter named James Marshall was building a sawmill along the American River in California. The mill's owner was John Sutter, a European immigrant from Switzerland.

On January 24, 1848, Marshall saw something in the water at the mill. It was a gold nugget. Once word of his find

During the gold rush of 1849, thousands of people took the California Trail. Sutter's Mill (above) drew large numbers of gold seekers.

California or Oregon?

Many people believed that money-hungry troublemakers went to California. They believed that educated and well-mannered people went to Oregon. These beliefs were not necessarily true.

got out, people entered the area. The biggest rush started in 1849, so gold hunters got the name 49ers. People arrived from all over the world to find wealth.

Over the next few years, California's population increased very rapidly. In 1848, about 15,000 people lived there. By the end of 1849, there were more than 100,000 people. By 1852, 250,000 people lived in California.

Finding Gold Was Hard Work

Many gold hunters did not realize that prospecting was a difficult and dangerous job. Many people found the difficult trip to California easier than the search for gold itself. At the crowded, filthy mining camps, miners sometimes died of accidents, disease, and poor food. In one camp, one out of five miners died in a six-month period.

Hard work also did not necessarily mean success. Many people spent endless days in an icy mountain river separating gold from dirt. Some prospectors became rich, but most went home poor.

The gold rush brought out the worst in many people. So great was gold fever that some people simply left their family or job to seek their fortune. Most people came to California only to take gold and leave. They did not plan on staying.

Other people settled into a new life in California as farmers or ranchers. Some made a fortune by selling goods and services to the mobs of

Many prospectors did not realize how hard it would be to hunt for gold.

Levi's Jeans

Originally from Germany, Levi Strauss moved from New York to San Francisco during the California gold rush. With Jacob Davis, Strauss took men's work pants and placed rivets, or metal pins, at weak points. Gold miners liked the pants because they lasted longer than other pants. These "waist overalls," as jeans were first called, made Strauss rich. Levi's jeans are still sold today.

gold seekers. The towns around Sutter's Mill grew from small settlements to busy cities in a short time.

The Donner Party

The California portion of the Oregon Trail was dangerous. The Donner Party clearly demonstrated this fact. The group became famous for the worst tragedy of the westward migration.

In 1846, shortly before the gold rush began, Lansford Hastings published *The Emigrant's Guide to Oregon and California.* The Hastings guide described a short route to California that cut through Utah and Nevada. The guide convinced a group of emigrants, including the Reed and Donner families, to take the shortcut that year. The Hastings guide did not say the route was untested.

Taking the Shortcut

People warned against the shortcut. One man said wagons could not make it through the trail. The man said the group would die if they left the known, safer route. James Reed, a member of the party, insisted that the group take the shortcut. Near South Pass, the group left the Oregon Trail for the shortcut.

The shortcut was difficult. First, the group had to cut through heavily wooded mountains. They averaged just over 2 miles (3 kilometers) per day. A normal day's travel should have been about 10 to 15 miles (16 to 24 kilometers). Then, the group crossed a desert that was wider than they had believed. People and oxen died of thirst.

Winter for the Donner Party

Because of the shortcut's difficulties, the group was late in reaching the Sierra Nevadas. Supplies were running low. The worst blizzard ever recorded in the Sierra Nevadas trapped the group high in the

Rescuers set out from Sutter's Fort to save the Donner Party, shown here in the winter of 1846–1847.

The Wealthy Reeds

The wealthy Reed family built a two-story wagon with a stove, spring-cushioned seats, and sleeping bunks. Eight oxen were needed to pull it. Virginia Reed, age 12, called it their "pioneer palace car."

mountains. The party made huts and cabins and waited out the winter.

The group starved, and many members died of hunger. Some of those left alive began eating the dead to survive.

In December 1846, 15 of the strongest survivors left to find help in California. Only seven made it to Sutter's Fort in California a month later. Over the next two months, the fort sent four rescue parties. The rescuers faced dangers and awful storms to save the starving emigrants.

Of 87 people in the Donner party, almost half died. The Donner family alone lost four adults and four children. The story of the Donner tragedy spread quickly. Emigrants avoided California for a time, and the shortcut was abandoned.

Chapter Five

Connecting Coast to Coast

Near the end of the Oregon Trail, emigrants moved as fast as they could, but they remained especially careful. They even boiled their drinking water to keep themselves from getting sick. They wanted to be sure nothing happened to them when their goal was so close. At trail's end in Oregon City, the wagon trains broke up, and the individuals started their new lives.

The United States and Britain signed the Oregon Treaty of 1846. In the treaty, Britain gave up its claims to Oregon south of the 49th parallel. That line marked the boundary between much of the western United States and Canada. The treaty was like a signal for U.S. citizens to pour into the area.

In 1848, Oregon officially became the Oregon Territory. In 1859, it became the 33rd state.

Thousands of emigrants traveled in wagons like those above.
People poured into the Oregon Territory starting in the 1840s.

The Mexican War

In 1846, the United States tried to buy California from Mexico, which claimed that area. Mexico refused to sell.

That same year, the U.S. government declared war on Mexico because it was blocking the U.S. westward expansion. The U.S. Army invaded Mexico. The painting below shows the Battle of Chapultepec, a fort near Mexico City.

In 1848, a peace treaty between the two countries ended the war. The United States paid Mexico $15 million. In return, Mexico gave up modern-day Arizona, New Mexico, California, Nevada, Utah, western Colorado, and part of Texas. Mexico no longer barred the way to the West's ports and natural riches.

The Transcontinental Railroad

The United States now controlled California, Oregon, and much of central North America. The U.S. government saw a need to connect this huge area by means of a coast-to-coast rail system.

For years, many people argued about the best rail route. Finally, the U.S. Congress chose a route. On July 1, 1862, President Abraham Lincoln signed the Pacific Railroad Act.

The act signaled the start of fierce competition between two railroad companies. The Union Pacific laid track west across the Great Plains starting at Omaha, Nebraska. The Central Pacific started at Sacramento, California, and laid track east through the Sierra Nevadas. The U.S. government paid each company based on how much track it laid.

On May 10, 1869, the Union Pacific and Central Pacific Railroads joined at Promontory Point, Utah. The connection bridged the West from the Mississippi River to the Pacific Ocean. It shortened the East-West trip from six months to six days. Eventually, seven transcontinental rail routes were built.

Chapter Six

Grabbing Opportunity

Railroad construction increased settlement and development of the West. The Pacific states quickly grew, and western life gradually became more like life in the East.

Many people think that the completion of the transcontinental railroad in 1869 ended the need for the Oregon Trail. Wagon traffic did slow down, but rail travel still was too expensive for many families. Covered wagons were slow, but they were cheap. The last wagons westward arrived in Oregon in 1914.

In some parts of the Oregon Trail, tracks from wagons that passed a hundred years ago are still visible today. The tracks above are at South Pass.

Ezra Meeker

Ezra Meeker was one of thousands of U.S. emigrants to travel to Oregon. At age 76, Meeker decided to make the trip again—in the opposite direction.

In 1902, Meeker loaded a wagon, bought some oxen, and retraced the trail from Oregon eastward. His purpose was to encourage preservation of the trail. He placed markers at historic spots and raised money to preserve what was still left of the Oregon Trail. He continued to promote the trail until his death at age 98.

The western migration encouraged the development of characteristics that people often consider American. The migration promoted national pride. This happened because emigrant movement made people less attached to specific regions and more attached to "being American."

The Effects of the Trail

The westward movement promoted hard work and hope for the future. To make their new lives work, emigrants had to be inventive and able to rely on themselves. People who went west were determined to survive and succeed. The Oregon Trail had served its purpose.

The Oregon Trail still exists. Parts of it can be seen in the form of wagon ruts, forts, and natural landmarks. Modern emigrants no longer cross North America in covered wagons to find new lives, but the trail still is an important part of U.S. history.

TIMELINE

Louisiana Purchase

Oregon agreement between the United States and Great Britain

The Donner Party begins its journey; Mexican War begins.

John Frémont's first western expedition

The Great Migration

| 1803 | 1812 | 1842 | 1843 | 1846 |

Lewis and Clark prepare to leave on expedition. They return in 1806.

United States and Britain sign the Oregon Treaty

Oregon country organized
into Oregon Territory;
Mexican War ends.

James Beckwourth
discovers the Beckwourth
Pass in Sierra Nevadas.

U.S. Civil War begins. It
ends in 1865.

| 1848 | 1849 | 1850 | 1859 | 1861 | 1862 | 1914 |

The California Gold
Rush begins.

Oregon becomes
the 33rd state.

The last
covered wagon
goes to Oregon.

Transcontinental
railroad built.
Completed in 1869.

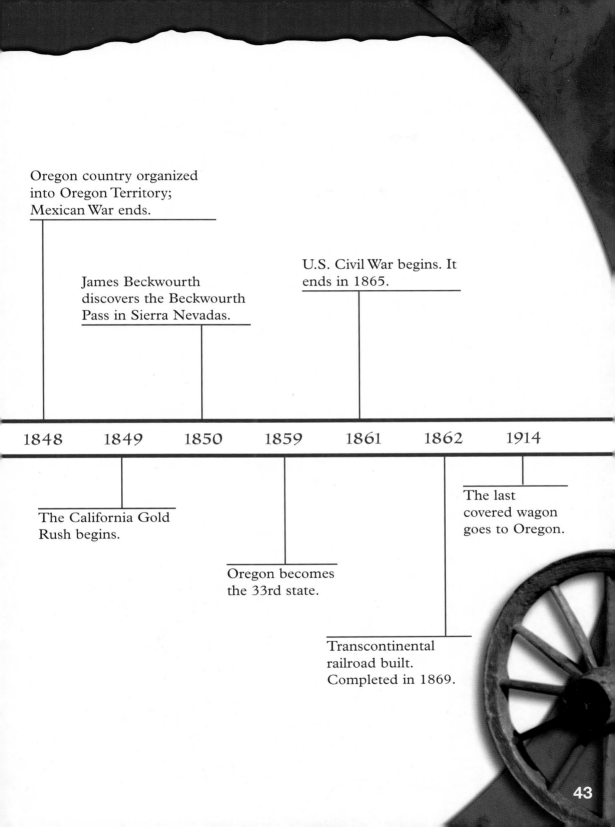

Glossary

Continental Divide (kon-tuh-NENT-uhl di-VIDE)—high point of North America; the rivers on the west of the divide flow toward the Pacific Ocean; the rivers on the east flow toward the Gulf of Mexico.

emigrant (EM-uh-gruhnt)—a person who leaves one place to live in another; many emigrants left U.S. territory to move to Oregon Country or California.

go-back (GOH-bak)—an emigrant who decided to leave the Oregon Trail and head back home to the East

gold rush (GOHLD RUHSH)—huge migration in 1849 to a site in California where gold was discovered

migration (mye-GRAY-shuhn)—a movement of people from one area to another

missionary (MISH-uh-ner-ee)—a member of a religious group who teaches the group's faith in a foreign country

prairie (PRAIR-ee)—a large stretch of flat or rolling grassland with few or no trees

prairie schooner (PRAIR-ee SKOO-nur)—a covered wagon used to travel across the Oregon Trail

prospector (PROSS-pek-tur)—a person who hunts for gold

transcontinental railroad (transs-kon-tuh-NEN-tuhl RAYL-rohd)—a railroad that connected the East Coast to the West Coast of the United States

wagon train (WAG-uhn TRANE)—a group of covered wagons that traveled together on a long trip West

For Further Reading

Blackwood, Gary L. *Life on the Oregon Trail.* The Way People Live. San Diego: Lucent Books, 1999.

Blashfield, Jean F. *The Oregon Trail.* We the People. Minneapolis: Compass Point Books, 2001.

Burger, James P. *The Oregon Trail.* The Library of Westward Expansion. New York: PowerKids Press, 2002.

Calabro, Marian. *The Perilous Journey of the Donner Party.* New York: Clarion Books, 1999.

Green, Carl R. *The California Trail to Gold in American History.* Berkeley Heights, N.J.: Enslow, 2000.

Hester, Sallie. *A Covered-Wagon Girl: The Diary of Sallie Hester, 1849–1850.* Diaries, Letters, and Memoirs. Christy Steele and Ann Hodgson, eds. Mankato, Minn.: Blue Earth Books, 2000.

Stefoff, Rebecca. *The Oregon Trail in American History.* In American History. Springfield, N.J.: Enslow, 1997.

Places of Interest

Museum of the City of San Francisco
945 Taraval Street
San Francisco, CA 94116
Museum of San Francisco history

Museum of Western Expansion Tour
Jefferson National Expansion
Memorial
11 North Fourth Street
St. Louis, MO 63102
*http://www.nps.gov/jeff/
mus-tour.htm*
St. Louis park that includes the
Arch monument as well as the
Old Courthouse and the Museum
of Westward Expansion

The National Frontier Trails Center
318 West Pacific Avenue
Independence, MO 64050
*http://www.frontiertrailscenter.
com*
Stories and exhibits about the
most popular jumping-off city for
the Oregon Trail

The National Oregon/California Trail Center
320 North Fourth Street
Montpelier, ID 83254
http://www.oregontrailcenter.org
Living history center dedicated to
the Oregon-California Trail in
Idaho, located at the "Clover
Creek Encampment"; emigrants
rested here after the steep descent
down Big Hill; wheel ruts from
their wagons can still be seen.

Whitman Mission National Historic Site
Route 2
Walla Walla, WA 99362
The trail as it passes the
original Christian mission to the
Cayuse Indians

Internet Sites

Do you want to learn more about the Oregon Trail?
Visit the FactHound at *www.facthound.com*

FactHound can track down many sites to help you. All the
FactHound sites are hand-selected by our editors. FactHound will
fetch the best, most accurate information to answer your questions.

IT'S EASY! IT'S FUN!
1) Go to *www.facthound.com*
2) Type in: **073681101X**
3) Click on **FETCH IT** and FactHound will put you on the trail
   of several helpful links.

You can also search by subject or book title. So, relax
and let our pal FactHound do the research for you!

Index